Skillstreaming
the Elementary School Child

Program
Forms

New Strategies and Perspectives for Teaching Prosocial Skills

Ellen McGinnis
Arnold P. Goldstein

Research Press • 2612 North Mattis Avenue • Champaign, Illinois 61822
www.researchpress.com

CONTENTS

Student:_____ Class/age: _____

Teacher/staff: _____ Date: _____

INSTRUCTIONS: Listed below you will find a number of skills that children are more or less proficient in using. This checklist will help you evaluate how well each child uses the various skills. For each child, rate his/her use of each skill, based on your observations of the his/her behavior in various situations.

Circle 1 if the child is *almost never* good at using the skill.
Circle 2 if the child is *seldom* good at using the skill.
Circle 3 if the child is *sometimes* good at using the skill.
Circle 4 if the child is *often* good at using the skill.
Circle 5 if the child is *almost always* good at using the skill.

Please rate the child on all skills listed. If you know of a situation in which the child has particular difficulty in using the skill well, please note it briefly in the space marked "Problem situation."

	almost never	seldom	sometimes	often	almost always

1. **Listening:** Does the student appear to listen when someone is speaking and make an effort to understand what is said?   1 2 3 4 5

   Problem situation:

2. **Asking for Help:** Does the student decide when he/she needs assistance and ask for this help in a pleasant manner?   1 2 3 4 5

   Problem situation:

3. **Saying Thank You:** Does the student tell others he/she appreciates help given, favors, and so forth?   1 2 3 4 5

   Problem situation:

	almost never	seldom	sometimes	often	almost always

4. **Bringing Materials to Class:** Does the student remember the books and materials he/she needs for class?

    1   2   3   4   5

Problem situation:

5. **Following Instructions:** Does the student understand instructions and follow them?

    1   2   3   4   5

Problem situation:

6. **Completing Assignments:** Does the student complete assignments at his/her independent academic level?

    1   2   3   4   5

Problem situation:

7. **Contributing to Discussions:** Does the student participate in class discussions in accordance with classroom rules?

    1   2   3   4   5

Problem situation:

8. **Offering Help to an Adult:** Does the student offer to help you at appropriate times and in an appropriate manner?

    1   2   3   4   5

Problem situation:

9. **Asking a Question:** Does the student know how and when to ask a question of another person?

    1   2   3   4   5

Problem situation:

10. **Ignoring Distractions:** Does the student ignore classroom distractions?

           1   2   3   4   5

    Problem situation:

11. **Making Corrections:** Does the student make the necessary corrections on assignments without getting overly frustrated?

           1   2   3   4   5

    Problem situation:

12. **Deciding on Something to Do:** Does the student find something to do when he/she has free time?

           1   2   3   4   5

    Problem situation:

13. **Setting a Goal:** Does the student set realistic goals for himself/herself and take the necessary steps to meet these goals?

           1   2   3   4   5

    Problem situation:

14. **Introducing Yourself:** Does the student introduce himself/herself in an appropriate way to people he/she doesn't know?

           1   2   3   4   5

    Problem situation:

15. **Beginning a Conversation:** Does the student know how and when to begin a conversation with another person?

           1   2   3   4   5

    Problem situation:

16. **Ending a Conversation:** Does the student end a conversation when it is necessary and in an appropriate manner?   1 2 3 4 5

Problem situation:

17. **Joining In:** Does the student know and practice acceptable ways of joining an ongoing activity or group?   1 2 3 4 5

Problem situation:

18. **Playing a Game:** Does the student play games with classmates fairly?   1 2 3 4 5

Problem situation:

19. **Asking a Favor:** Does the student know how to ask a favor of another person?   1 2 3 4 5

Problem situation:

20. **Offering Help to a Classmate:** Can the student recognize when someone needs or wants assistance and offer this help?   1 2 3 4 5

Problem situation:

21. **Giving a Compliment:** Does the student tell others that he/she likes something about them or something they have done?   1 2 3 4 5

Problem situation:

| | almost never | seldom | sometimes | often | almost always |

22. **Accepting a Compliment:** Does the student accept these comments given by adults or his/her peers in a friendly way?

    1   2   3   4   5

Problem situation:

23. **Suggesting an Activity:** Does the student suggest appropriate activities to others?

    1   2   3   4   5

Problem situation:

24. **Sharing:** Is the student agreeable to sharing things with others and, if not, does he/she offer acceptable reasons for not sharing?

    1   2   3   4   5

Problem situation:

25. **Apologizing:** Does the student tell others sincerely that he/she is sorry for doing something?

    1   2   3   4   5

Problem situation:

26. **Knowing Your Feelings:** Does the student identify feelings he/she is experiencing?

    1   2   3   4   5

Problem situation:

27. **Expressing Your Feelings:** Does the student express his/her feelings in acceptable ways?

    1   2   3   4   5

Problem situation:

28. **Recognizing Another's Feelings:** Does the student try to figure out in acceptable ways how others are feeling? 1 2 3 4 5

    Problem situation:

29. **Showing Understanding of Another's Feelings:** Does the student show understanding of others' feelings in acceptable ways? 1 2 3 4 5

    Problem situation:

30. **Expressing Concern for Another:** Does the student express concern for others in acceptable ways? 1 2 3 4 5

    Problem situation:

31. **Dealing with Your Anger:** Does the student use acceptable ways to express his/her anger? 1 2 3 4 5

    Problem situation:

32. **Dealing with Another's Anger:** Does the student try to understand another's anger without getting angry himself/herself? 1 2 3 4 5

    Problem situation:

33. **Expressing Affection:** Does the student let others know in acceptable ways that he/she cares about them? 1 2 3 4 5

    Problem situation:

34. **Dealing with Fear:** Does the student know why he/she is afraid and practice strategies to reduce this fear?

almost never 1 seldom 2 sometimes 3 often 4 almost always 5

Problem situation:

35. **Rewarding Yourself:** Does the student say and do nice things for himself/herself when a reward is deserved?

1 2 3 4 5

Problem situation:

36. **Using Self-Control:** Does the student know and practice strategies to control his/her temper or excitement?

1 2 3 4 5

Problem situation:

37. **Asking Permission:** Does the student know when and how to ask whether he/she may do something?

1 2 3 4 5

Problem situation:

38. **Responding to Teasing:** Does the student deal with being teased in ways that allow him/her to remain in control?

1 2 3 4 5

Problem situation:

39. **Avoiding Trouble:** Does the student stay away from situations that may get him/her into trouble?

1 2 3 4 5

Problem situation:

40. **Staying Out of Fights:** Does the student know of and practice socially appropriate ways of handling potential fights?

    1   2   3   4   5

Problem situation:

41. **Problem Solving:** When a problem occurs, does the student think of alternatives, choose an alternative, then evaluate how well this solved the problem?

    1   2   3   4   5

Problem situation:

42. **Accepting Consequences:** Does the student accept the consequences for his/her behavior without becoming defensive or upset?

    1   2   3   4   5

Problem situation:

43. **Dealing with an Accusation:** Does the student know of and practice ways to deal with being accused of something?

    1   2   3   4   5

Problem situation:

44. **Negotiating:** Is the student willing to give and take in order to reach a compromise?

    1   2   3   4   5

Problem situation:

45. **Dealing with Boredom:** Does the student select acceptable activities when he/she is bored?

    1   2   3   4   5

Problem situation:

46. **Deciding What Caused a Problem:** Does the student assess what caused a problem and accept responsibility if appropriate?

     1 2 3 4 5

    Problem situation:

47. **Making a Complaint:** Does the student know how to express disagreement in acceptable ways?

     1 2 3 4 5

    Problem situation:

48. **Answering a Complaint:** Is the student willing to arrive at a fair solution to someone's justified complaint?

     1 2 3 4 5

    Problem situation:

49. **Dealing with Losing:** Does the student accept losing at a game or activity without becoming upset or angry?

     1 2 3 4 5

    Problem situation:

50. **Being a Good Sport:** Does the student give a sincere compliment to others about how they played a game?

     1 2 3 4 5

    Problem situation:

51. **Dealing with Being Left Out:** Does the student deal with being left out of an activity without losing control?

     1 2 3 4 5

    Problem situation:

52. **Dealing with Embarrassment:** Does the student know of things to do that help him/her feel less embarrassed or self-conscious?   1   2   3   4   5

Problem situation:

53. **Reacting to Failure:** Does the student figure out reason(s) for his/her failure and ways to be more successful the next time?   1   2   3   4   5

Problem situation:

54. **Accepting No:** Does the student accept being told no without becoming unduly upset or angry?   1   2   3   4   5

Problem situation:

55. **Saying No:** Does the student say no in acceptable ways to things he/she doesn't want to do or to things that may get him/her into trouble?   1   2   3   4   5

Problem situation:

56. **Relaxing:** Is the student able to relax when tense or upset?   1   2   3   4   5

Problem situation:

57. **Dealing with Group Pressure:** Does the student decide what he/she wants to do when others pressure him/her to do something else?   1   2   3   4   5

Problem situation:

58. **Dealing with Wanting Something That Isn't Yours:** Does the student refrain from taking things that don't belong to him/her?

        1   2   3   4   5

    Problem situation:

59. **Making a Decision:** Does the student make thoughtful choices?

        1   2   3   4   5

    Problem situation:

60. **Being Honest:** Is the student honest when confronted with a negative action?

        1   2   3   4   5

    Problem situation:

Name: _____ Date: _____

Child's name: _____ Birth date: _____

INSTRUCTIONS: Based on your observations in various situations, rate your child's use of the following skills.

Circle 1 if the child is *almost never* good at using the skill.
Circle 2 if the child is *seldom* good at using the skill.
Circle 3 if the child is *sometimes* good at using the skill.
Circle 4 if the child is *often* good at using the skill.
Circle 5 if the child is *almost always* good at using the skill.

	almost never	seldom	sometimes	often	almost always
1. **Listening:** Does your child listen when you or others talk to him/her? Comments:	1	2	3	4	5
2. **Asking for Help:** Does your child decide when he/she needs assistance and ask for this help in a pleasant manner? Comments:	1	2	3	4	5
3. **Saying Thank You:** Does your child tell others he/she appreciates help given, favors, and so forth? Comments:	1	2	3	4	5
4. **Bringing Materials to Class:** Does your child remember the books and materials he/she needs for school? Comments:	1	2	3	4	5

5. **Following Instructions:** Does your child understand instructions and follow them?

   Comments:

6. **Completing Assignments:** Does your child complete his/her homework assignments?

   Comments:

   1   2   3   4   5

7. **Contributing to Discussions:** Does your child participate in class discussions in accordance with classroom rules?

   Comments:

   1   2   3   4   5

8. **Offering Help to an Adult:** Does your child offer to help you at appropriate times and in an appropriate manner?

   Comments:

   1   2   3   4   5

9. **Asking a Question:** Does your child know how and when to ask a question of another person?

   Comments:

   1   2   3   4   5

10. **Ignoring Distractions:** Does your child ignore distractions in order to get his/her work done?

    Comments:

    1   2   3   4   5

11. **Making Corrections:** Does your child make the necessary corrections on assignments without getting overly frustrated?

    1   2   3   4   5

Comments:

12. **Deciding on Something to Do:** Does your child find something to do when he/she has free time?

    1   2   3   4   5

Comments:

13. **Setting a Goal:** Does your child set realistic goals for himself/herself and take the necessary steps to meet these goals?

    1   2   3   4   5

Comments:

14. **Introducing Yourself:** Does your child introduce himself/herself in an appropriate way to people he/she doesn't know?

    1   2   3   4   5

Comments:

15. **Beginning a Conversation:** Does your child know how and when to begin a conversation with another person?

    1   2   3   4   5

Comments:

16. **Ending a Conversation:** Does your child end a conversation when it is necessary and in an appropriate manner?

    1   2   3   4   5

Comments:

17. **Joining In:** Does your child know and practice acceptable ways of joining an ongoing activity or group?

1 2 3 4 5

Comments:

18. **Playing a Game:** Does your child play games with friends fairly?

1 2 3 4 5

Comments:

19. **Asking a Favor:** Does your child know how to ask a favor of another person in an appropriate way?

1 2 3 4 5

Comments:

20. **Offering Help to a Classmate:** Does your child recognize when someone needs or wants assistance and offer this help?

1 2 3 4 5

Comments:

21. **Giving a Compliment:** Does your child tell others that he/she likes something about them or something they have done?

1 2 3 4 5

Comments:

22. **Accepting a Compliment:** Does your child accept compliments given by adults or his/her peers in a friendly way?

1 2 3 4 5

Comments:

23. **Suggesting an Activity:** Does your child suggest appropriate activities to others?

       1   2   3   4   5

Comments:

24. **Sharing:** Is your child agreeable to sharing things with others and, if not, does he/she offer acceptable reasons for not sharing?

       1   2   3   4   5

Comments:

25. **Apologizing:** Does your child tell others sincerely that he/she is sorry for doing something?

       1   2   3   4   5

Comments:

26. **Knowing Your Feelings:** Does your child identify feelings he/she is experiencing?

       1   2   3   4   5

Comments:

27. **Expressing Your Feelings:** Does your child express his/her feelings in acceptable ways?

       1   2   3   4   5

Comments:

28. **Recognizing Another's Feelings:** Does your child try to figure out in acceptable ways how others are feeling?

       1   2   3   4   5

Comments:

29. **Showing Understanding of Another's Feelings:** Does your child show understanding of others' feelings in acceptable ways?

      1 2 3 4 5

Comments:

30. **Expressing Concern for Another:** Does your child express concern for others in acceptable ways?

      1 2 3 4 5

Comments:

31. **Dealing with Your Anger:** Does your child use acceptable ways to express his/her anger?

      1 2 3 4 5

Comments:

32. **Dealing with Another's Anger:** Does your child try to understand another's anger without getting angry himself/herself?

      1 2 3 4 5

Comments:

33. **Expressing Affection:** Does your child let others know in acceptable ways that he/she cares about them?

      1 2 3 4 5

Comments:

34. **Dealing with Fear:** Does your child know why he/she is afraid and do positive things to reduce this fear?

      1 2 3 4 5

Comments:

	almost never	seldom	sometimes	often	almost always

35. **Rewarding Yourself:** Does your child say and do nice things for himself/herself when a reward is deserved?

Comments:

               1   2   3   4   5

36. **Using Self-Control:** Does your child know and use positive ways to control his/her temper or excitement?

Comments:

               1   2   3   4   5

37. **Asking Permission:** Does your child know when and how to ask whether he/she may do something?

Comments:

               1   2   3   4   5

38. **Responding to Teasing:** Does your child deal with being teased without losing control?

Comments:

               1   2   3   4   5

39. **Avoiding Trouble:** Does your child stay away from situations that may get him/her into trouble?

Comments:

               1   2   3   4   5

40. **Staying Out of Fights:** Does your child know of and practice socially appropriate ways of handling potential fights?

Comments:

               1   2   3   4   5

41. **Problem Solving:** When a problem occurs, does your child think of alternatives, choose an alternative, then evaluate how well this solved the problem?

    1 2 3 4 5

    Comments:

42. **Accepting Consequences:** Does your child accept the consequences for his/her behavior without becoming defensive or upset?

    1 2 3 4 5

    Comments:

43. **Dealing with an Accusation:** Does your child deal in positive ways with being accused of something?

    1 2 3 4 5

    Comments:

44. **Negotiating:** Is your child willing to give and take in order to reach a compromise?

    1 2 3 4 5

    Comments:

45. **Dealing with Boredom:** Does your child select acceptable activities when he/she is bored?

    1 2 3 4 5

    Comments:

46. **Deciding What Caused a Problem:** Does your child assess what caused a problem and accept responsibility if appropriate?

    1 2 3 4 5

    Comments:

47. **Making a Complaint:** Does your child know how to express disagreement in acceptable ways?

    1   2   3   4   5

    Comments:

48. **Answering a Complaint:** Is your child willing to arrive at a fair solution to someone's justified complaint?

    1   2   3   4   5

    Comments:

49. **Dealing with Losing:** Does your child accept losing at a game or activity without becoming upset or angry?

    1   2   3   4   5

    Comments:

50. **Being a Good Sport:** Does your child give a sincere compliment to others about how they played a game?

    1   2   3   4   5

    Comments:

51. **Dealing with Being Left Out:** Does your child deal with being left out of an activity without losing control?

    1   2   3   4   5

    Comments:

52. **Dealing with Embarrassment:** Does your child know of things to do that help him/her feel less embarrassed or self-conscious?

    1   2   3   4   5

    Comments:

53. **Reacting to Failure:** Does your child figure out the reason(s) for his/her failure and ways he/she can be more successful the next time?

    Comments:

        1   2   3   4   5

54. **Accepting No:** Does your child accept being told no without becoming unduly upset or angry?

    Comments:

        1   2   3   4   5

55. **Saying No:** Does your child say no in acceptable ways to things he/she doesn't want to do or to things that may get him/her into trouble?

    Comments:

        1   2   3   4   5

56. **Relaxing:** Is your child able to relax when tense or upset?

    Comments:

        1   2   3   4   5

57. **Dealing with Group Pressure:** Does your child decide what he/she wants to do when others pressure him/her to do something else?

    Comments:

        1   2   3   4   5

58. **Dealing with Wanting Something That Isn't Yours:** Does your child refrain from taking things that don't belong to him/her?

    Comments:

	almost never	seldom	sometimes	often	almost always

59. **Making a Decision:** Does your child make thoughtful choices?

         1   2   3   4   5

Comments:

60. **Being Honest:** Is your child honest when confronted with a negative action?

         1   2   3   4   5

Comments:

Student Skillstreaming Checklist

Name: _____ Date: _____

INSTRUCTIONS: Each of the questions will ask you about how well you do something.
Next to each question is a number.

Circle number 1 if you *almost never* do what the question asks.
Circle number 2 if you *seldom* do it.
Circle number 3 if you *sometimes* do it.
Circle number 4 if you do it *often.*
Circle number 5 if you *almost always* do it.

There are no right or wrong answers to these questions.
Answer the way you really feel about each question.

	almost never	seldom	sometimes	often	almost always
1. Is it easy for me to listen to someone who is talking to me?	1	2	3	4	5
2. Do I ask for help in a friendly way when I need help?	1	2	3	4	5
3. Do I tell people thank you for something they have done for me?	1	2	3	4	5
4. Do I have the materials I need for my classes (like books, pencils, paper)?	1	2	3	4	5
5. Do I understand what to do when directions are given, and do I follow these directions?	1	2	3	4	5
6. Do I finish my schoolwork?	1	2	3	4	5
7. Do I join in on class talks or discussions?	1	2	3	4	5
8. Do I try to help an adult when I think he/she could use the help?	1	2	3	4	5
9. Do I decide what I don't understand about my schoolwork and ask my teacher questions in a friendly way?	1	2	3	4	5
10. Is it easy for me to keep doing my schoolwork when people are noisy?	1	2	3	4	5

	almost never	seldom	sometimes	often	almost always

11. Do I fix mistakes on my work without getting upset?   1 2 3 4 5

12. Do I choose something to do when I have free time?   1 2 3 4 5

13. Do I decide on something I want to work for and keep working until I get it?   1 2 3 4 5

14. Is it easy for me to take the first step to meet somebody I don't know?   1 2 3 4 5

15. Is it easy for me to start a conversation with someone?   1 2 3 4 5

16. When I have something else I have to do, do I end a conversation with someone in a nice way?   1 2 3 4 5

17. Do I ask to join in a game or activity in a friendly way?   1 2 3 4 5

18. Do I follow the rules when I play a game?   1 2 3 4 5

19. Is it easy for me to ask a favor of someone?   1 2 3 4 5

20. Do I notice when somebody needs help and try to help the person?   1 2 3 4 5

21. Do I tell others that I like something nice about them or something nice they have done for me or for somebody else?   1 2 3 4 5

22. When someone says something nice about me, do I accept what the person says?   1 2 3 4 5

23. Do I suggest things to do with my friends?   1 2 3 4 5

24. Am I willing to share my things with others?   1 2 3 4 5

25. Do I tell others I'm sorry after I do something wrong?   1 2 3 4 5

26. Do I know how I feel about different things that happen?   1 2 3 4 5

27. Do I let others know what I am feeling and do it in a good way?   1 2 3 4 5

28. Do I try to tell how other people are feeling?   1 2 3 4 5

29. Do I show others that I understand how they feel?   1 2 3 4 5

30. When someone has a problem, do I let the person know that I care?   1 2 3 4 5

31. When I am angry, do I deal with it in ways that won't hurt other people? 1 2 3 4 5

32. Do I try to understand other people's angry feelings? 1 2 3 4 5

33. Do I let others know I care about them? 1 2 3 4 5

34. Do I know what makes me afraid, and do I think of things to do so I don't stay afraid? 1 2 3 4 5

35. Do I say and do nice things for myself when I have earned it? 1 2 3 4 5

36. Do I keep my temper when I am upset? 1 2 3 4 5

37. Do I know when I have to ask to do something I want to do, and do I ask in a friendly way? 1 2 3 4 5

38. When somebody teases me, do I stay in control? 1 2 3 4 5

39. Do I try to stay away from things that may get me into trouble? 1 2 3 4 5

40. Do I think of ways other than fighting to take care of problems? 1 2 3 4 5

41. Do I think of ways to deal with a problem and what might happen if I use these ways? 1 2 3 4 5

42. When I do something I shouldn't have done, do I accept what happens then? 1 2 3 4 5

43. Do I decide what I have been accused of and why, then think of a good way to handle the situation? 1 2 3 4 5

44. When I don't agree with somebody, do I help think of a plan to make both of us happy? 1 2 3 4 5

45. When I feel bored, do I think of good things to do and then do them? 1 2 3 4 5

46. Do I know when a problem happened because of something I did? 1 2 3 4 5

47. Do I tell others without getting mad or yelling when they have caused a problem for me? 1 2 3 4 5

	almost never	seldom	sometimes	often	almost always

48. Do I help think of a fair way to take care of a complaint against me? — 1 2 3 4 5

49. When I lose at a game, do I keep from getting upset? — 1 2 3 4 5

50. Do I tell others something good about the way they played a game? — 1 2 3 4 5

51. Do I decide if I have been left out, then do things in a good way to make me feel better? — 1 2 3 4 5

52. Do I do things that will help me feel less embarrassed? — 1 2 3 4 5

53. When I don't do well on something (on a test, doing my chores), do I decide ways I could do better next time? — 1 2 3 4 5

54. When I am told no, can I keep from becoming upset? — 1 2 3 4 5

55. Do I say no to things that might get me into trouble or that I don't want to do, and do I say it in a friendly way? — 1 2 3 4 5

56. Can I keep my body from getting tight and tense when I am angry or upset? — 1 2 3 4 5

57. When a group of kids wants me to do something that might get me into trouble or that is wrong, do I say no? — 1 2 3 4 5

58. Do I keep from taking things that aren't mine? — 1 2 3 4 5

59. Is it easy for me to decide what to do when I'm given a choice? — 1 2 3 4 5

60. Do I tell the truth about what I have done, even if I might get into trouble? — 1 2 3 4 5

student names

GROUP I
Classroom Survival Skills

1. Listening								
2. Asking for Help								
3. Saying Thank You								
4. Bringing Materials to Class								
5. Following Instructions								
6. Completing Assignments								
7. Contributing to Discussions								
8. Offering Help to an Adult								
9. Asking a Question								
10. Ignoring Distractions								
11. Making Corrections								
12. Deciding on Something to Do								
13. Setting a Goal								

GROUP II
Friendship-Making Skills

14. Introducing Yourself								
15. Beginning a Conversation								
16. Ending a Conversation								

	student names								
17. Joining In									
18. Playing a Game									
19. Asking a Favor									
20. Offering Help to a Classmate									
21. Giving a Compliment									
22. Accepting a Compliment									
23. Suggesting an Activity									
24. Sharing									
25. Apologizing									

GROUP III
Skills for Dealing with Feelings

26. Knowing Your Feelings									
27. Expressing Your Feelings									
28. Recognizing Another's Feelings									
29. Showing Understanding of Another's Feelings									
30. Expressing Concern for Another									
31. Dealing with Your Anger									
32. Dealing with Another's Anger									
33. Expressing Affection									

	student names								
34. Dealing with Fear									
35. Rewarding Yourself									
GROUP IV **Skill Alternatives to Aggression**									
36. Using Self-Control									
37. Asking Permission									
38. Responding to Teasing									
39. Avoiding Trouble									
40. Staying Out of Fights									
41. Problem Solving									
42. Accepting Consequences									
43. Dealing with an Accusation									
44. Negotiating									
GROUP V **Skills for Dealing with Stress**									
45. Dealing with Boredom									
46. Deciding What Caused a Problem									
47. Making a Complaint									
48. Answering a Complaint									
49. Dealing with Losing									

	student names								
50. Being a Good Sport									
51. Dealing with Being Left Out									
52. Dealing with Embarrassment									
53. Reacting to Failure									
54. Accepting No									
55. Saying No									
56. Relaxing									
57. Dealing with Group Pressure									
58. Dealing with Wanting Something That Isn't Yours									
59. Making a Decision									
60. Being Honest									

Name: _____ Date: _____

SKILL: _____

STEPS:

With whom will I try this?_____

When?_____

What happened?_____

_____

_____

How did I do?   ☺   😐   ☹

Why did I circle this? _____

_____

Name: _____ Date: _____

SKILL: _____

STEPS:

When did I practice?   How did I do?

_____

_____

_____

_____

Group Self-Report Chart

Skills

student names

35

School-Home Note

Student: _____ Date: _____

DESCRIPTION OF LESSON

Skill name: _____

Skill steps:

Skill purpose, use, value: _____

_____

DESCRIPTION OF SKILL HOMEWORK

_____

_____

REQUEST TO PARENTS

1. Provide skill homework recognition and reward.

2. Respond positively to your child's skill use.

3. Return this School-Home Note with your comments (on the back) about quality of homework done and questions/suggestions for the teacher.

4. Please sign and return this form to_____

   by _____

Signature: _____ Date: _____

Parent/Staff Skill Rating Form

Date: _____

_____ is learning
(student's name)

the skill of _____

The steps involved in this skill are:

1. Did he or she demonstrate this skill in your presence? ☐ yes   ☐ no

2. How would you rate his or her skill demonstration? *(check one)*

   ☐ poor   ☐ below average   ☐ average   ☐ above average   ☐ excellent

3. How sincere was he or she in performing the skill? *(check one)*

   ☐ not sincere   ☐ somewhat sincere   ☐ very sincere

Comments: _____

_____

_____

_____

Please sign and return this form to _____

by _____

Signature: _____ Date: _____

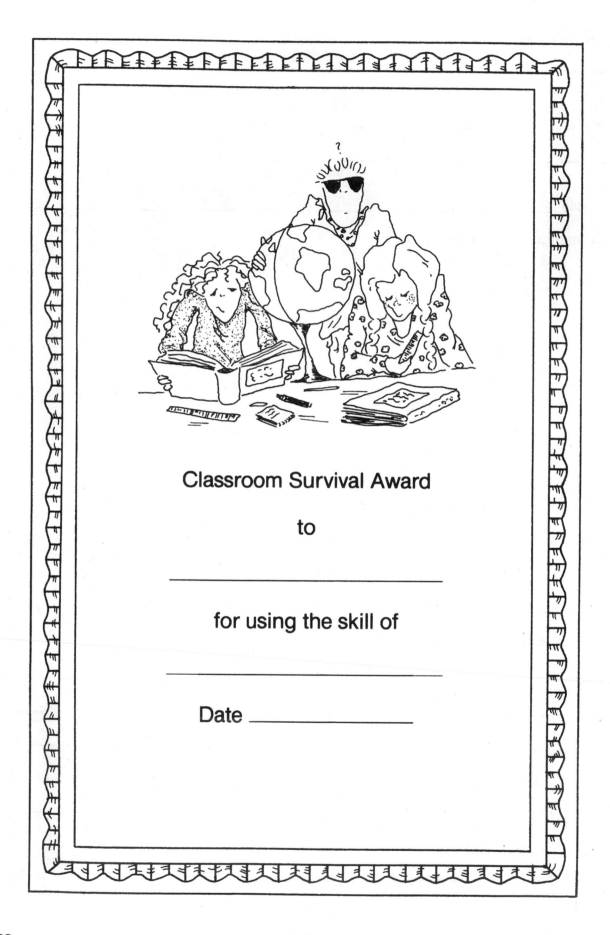

Classroom Survival Award

to

_____

for using the skill of

_____

Date _____

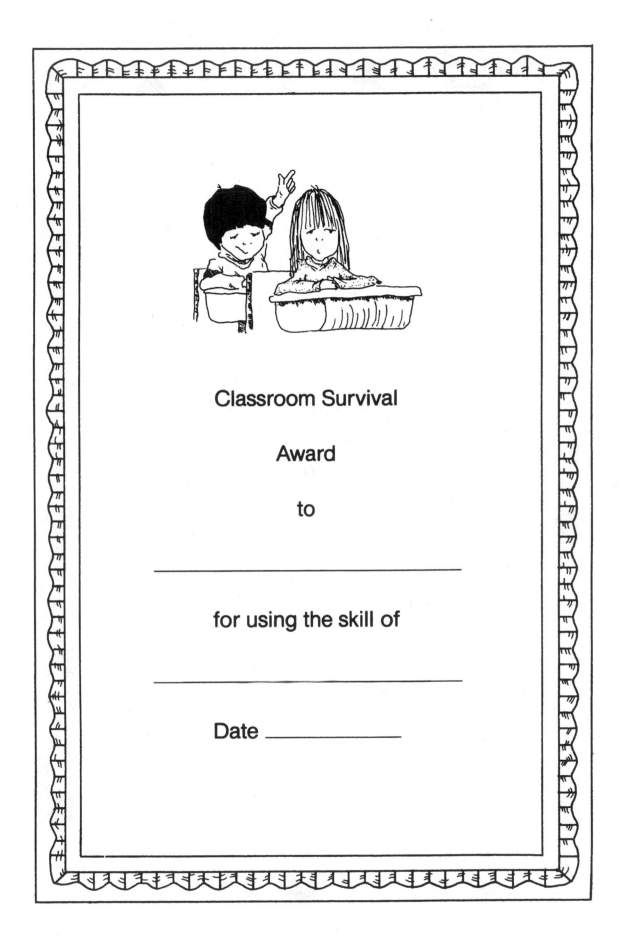

Classroom Survival

Award

to

_____

for using the skill of

_____

Date _____

Friendship Award

to

_____

for using the skill of

_____

Date _____

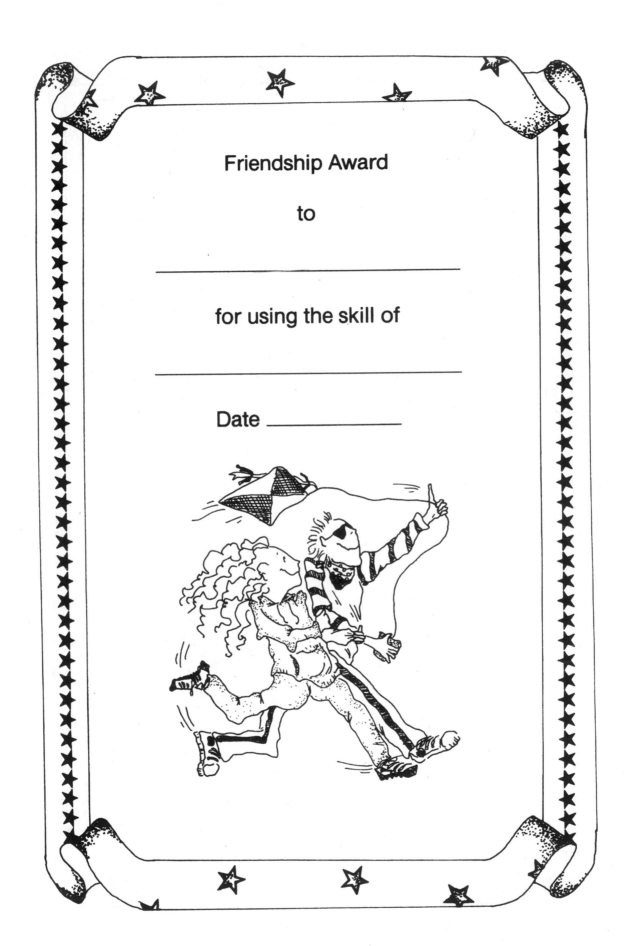

Friendship Award

to

_____

for using the skill of

_____

Date _____

Dealing with Stress Award

to

_____

for using the skill of

_____

Date _____

Dealing with Stress Award

to

_____

for using the skill of

_____

Date _____

Stop and Think Award

to

_____

for using the skill of

_____

Date _____

Stop and Think

Award

to

_____

for using the skill of

_____

Date _____

Dealing with Feelings Award

to

_____

for using the skill of

_____

Date _____

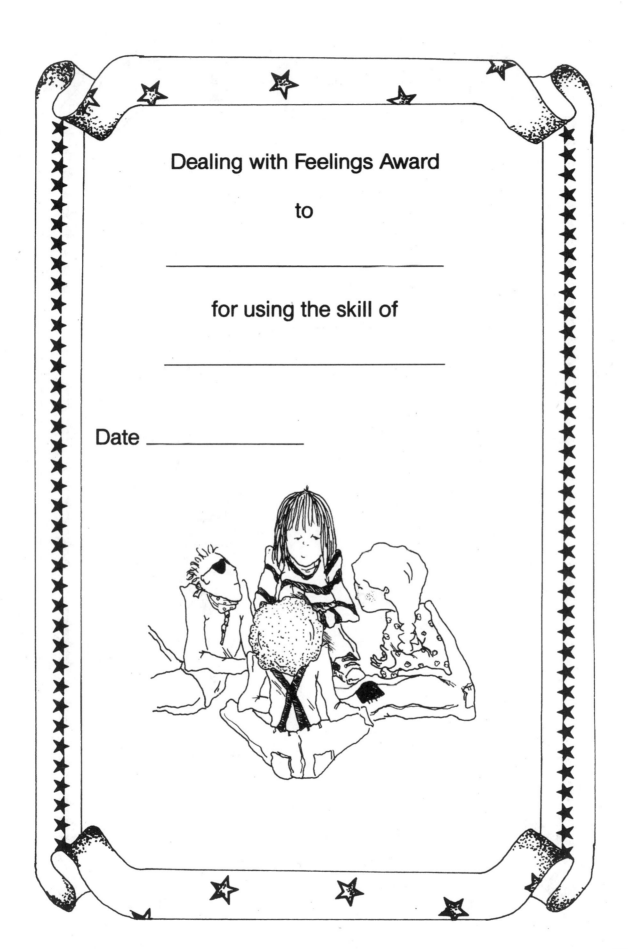

Dealing with Feelings Award

to

_____

for using the skill of

_____

Date _____

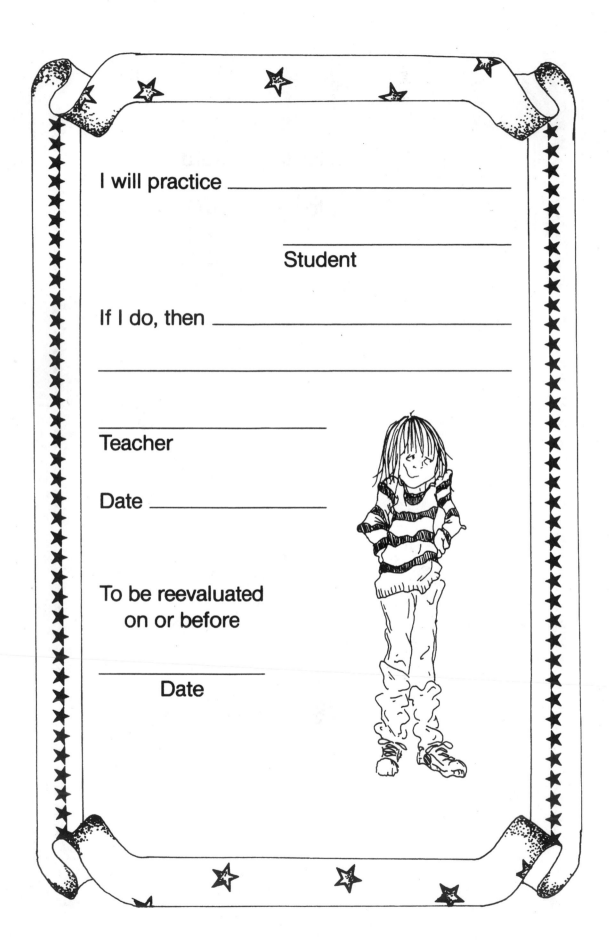

I will practice _____

_____
Student

If I do, then _____

_____

_____
Teacher

Date _____

To be reevaluated
on or before

_____
Date

My goal is to practice the skill of

_____

from _____ to _____
                    (dates)

If I do this, I will have earned

_____

_____

_____

Student _____

Teacher _____

Date _____

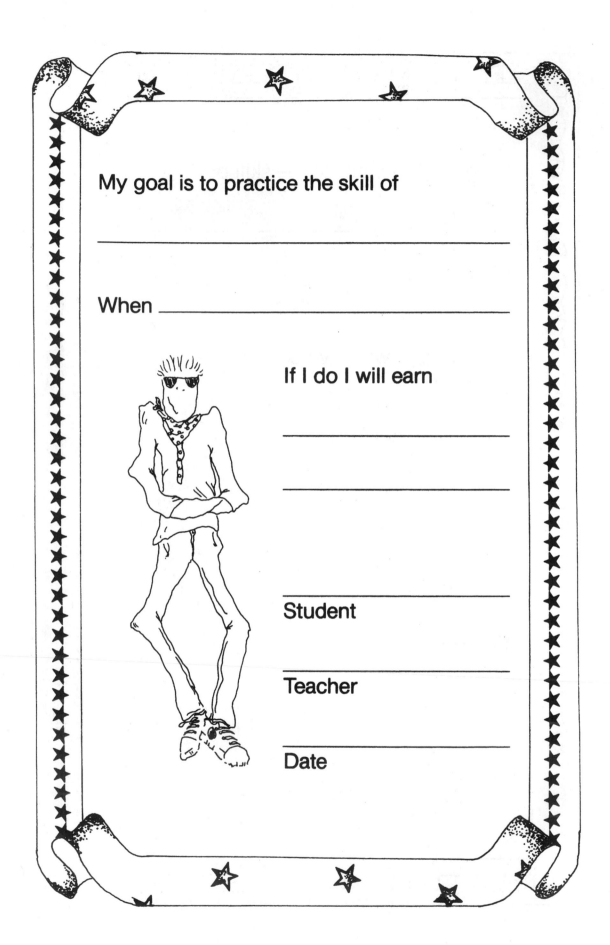

My goal is to practice the skill of

_____

When _____

If I do I will earn

_____

_____

_____

Student

_____

Teacher

_____

Date

50

I will _____

Then I can _____

Student   Teacher

_____   _____

Date _____

I will _____

Then I can _____

_____   _____
      Student   Teacher

Date _____

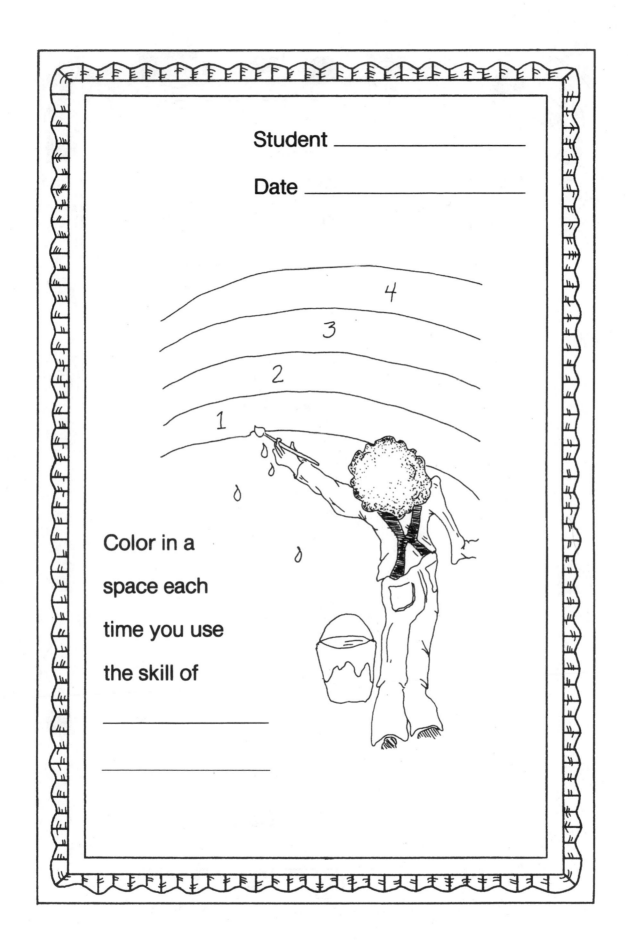

Student _____

Date _____

4

3

2

1

Color in a

space each

time you use

the skill of

_____

_____

Student _____

Color in a balloon each

time you use the skill of

_____

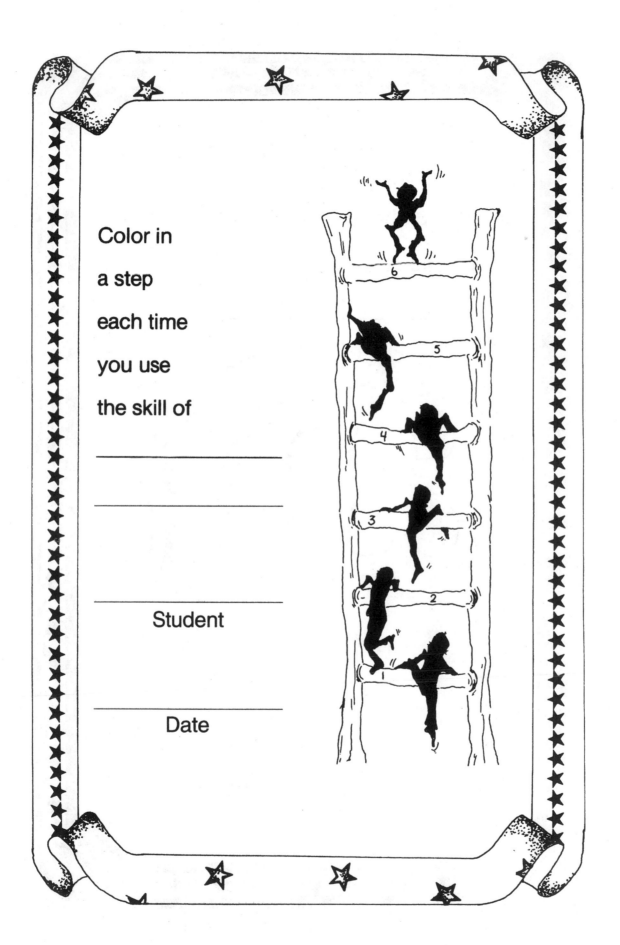

Color in

a step

each time

you use

the skill of

_____

_____

_____
Student

_____
Date

Student _____

Color a number each time

you practice the skill of

_____

Date _____